# 5 LET'S GO

4th Edition

STUDENT BOOK

**Ritsuko Nakata**

**Karen Frazier**

**Barbara Hoskins**

**songs and chants by Carolyn Graham**

OXFORD

UNIVERSITY PRESS

# OXFORD
## UNIVERSITY PRESS

198 Madison Avenue
New York, NY 10016 USA

Great Clarendon Street, Oxford, OX2 6DP, United Kingdom

Oxford University Press is a department of the University of Oxford.
It furthers the University's objective of excellence in research, scholarship,
and education by publishing worldwide. Oxford is a registered trade
mark of Oxford University Press in the UK and in certain other countries

General Manager, American ELT: Laura Pearson
Executive Publishing Manager: Shelagh Speers
Senior Managing Editor: Anne Stribling
Project Editor: June Schwartz
Art, Design, and Production Director: Susan Sanguily
Design Manager: Lisa Donovan
Designer: Sangeeta E. Ramcharan
Electronic Production Manager: Julie Armstrong
Production Artist: Elissa Santos
Image Manager: Trisha Masterson
Image Editor: Joe Kassner
Production Coordinator: Hila Ratzabi
Senior Manufacturing Controller: Eve Wong

ISBN: 978 0 19 462622 4 Student Book with Audio CD
ISBN: 978 0 19 464310 8 Student Book as pack component
ISBN: 978 0 19 464364 1 Audio CD as pack component

Printed in China

This book is printed on paper from certified and well-managed sources

ACKNOWLEDGEMENTS

*The authors and publisher are grateful to those who have given permission to reproduce
the following extracts and adaptations of copyright material:*

*Illustrations by:* Bernard Adnet: 45, 71(t); Lori Anzalone: 6(t), 9(c1, 2, 3, 4); Ilias
Arahovitis: 23(b); Fian Arroyo: 52(t), 63, 69(b); Ron Berg: 7, 8(t), 9(c5, 6, 7, 8),
69(t), 71(b); Beccy Blake: 35; Karen Brooks: 15(b), 29, 34(t), 41(t), 47, 50(t),
51(b), 56, 65; Mircea Catusanu: 5, 9(b), 16(t), 17, 20, 36, 37, 59, 60(t), 62(t), 74(t);
Daniel Del Valle: 51 (pictures on cork board); Fiammetta Dogi/The Art Agency:
10, 11(t), 14(t), 15(t); Daniel Griffo: 44 (b), 48, 50(b), 52(b), 58, 60(b), 62(b), 68(b),
70(b), and cats on pages 4, 6, 8, 10, 12, 14, 16, 18, 22, 24, 26, 28, 30, 32, 34, 36,
40, 42, 44, 46, 48, 50, 52, 54, 58, 60, 62, 64, 66, 68, 70 and 72; Richard Hoit:
13(b), 19, 43(b), 49, 53, 61, 64; David Lowe: 23(t), 26(t), 32(t), 33(t), 42(t), 43(t), 51
(boy and girl by cork board); Karen Minot: 54 (map), 67(t); Michael Morris: 2,
3, 4, 6(b), 8(b), 12, 14(b), 16(b), 22, 24(c), 26(b), 30, 32(b), 34(b); Keith Plechaty:
globes on pages 21, 39, 57 and 75; Sherry Rogers: 67(b), 72, 73; Maryn Roos:
iii, 74(b); Robert Roper: 27; Chris Vallo: 33(b), 41(b); Christina Wald: 55; Jason
Wolff: 11(b), 24(t), 25, 31, 38, 44(t); Josie Yee: 40, 42(b), 66.

*The publishers would like to thank the following for their kind permission to reproduce
photographs:* pg. 10Robert Red/shutterstock.com (font bkgd); pg. 10mark
huntington/istockphoto (fossil); pg. 10 Phil Degginger/Carnegie Museum/
Alamy (paleontologist); pg. 10-11 Borut Trdina/istockphoto.com (leaves);
pg. 11 AndreaAstes/istockphoto.com (fern); pg. 13 Dushenina/shutterstock.
com (wolf); pg. 13 Eric Isselée/istockphoto.com (zebra); pg. 13 Irving N
Saperstein/istockphoto.com (polar bear); pg. 13 Johan Swanepoel/istockphoto.
com (rhinoceros); pg. 13 Mike Dabell/istockphoto.com (gazelle); pg. 13 Gill
André/istockphoto.com (squirrel); pg. 13 Keith Barlow/istockphoto.com
(cheetah); pg. 13 First Light/Alamy (skunk); pg. 18 Eric Isselée/shutterstock.
com (zebra); pg. 18 Witold Kaszkin/shutterstock.com (polar bear); pg. 18 Mike
Truchon/shutterstock.com (hummingbird); pg. 18 Stubblefield Photography/
shutterstock.com (octopus); pg. 18 OceanwideImages.com (jellyfish); pg.
18-19 Andrew Simpson/istockphoto.com (fish bkgd); pg. 19 Jiri Vaclavek/
shutterstock.com (jellyfish); pg. 21 mary416/shutterstock.com (pandas eating);
pg. 21 Jim Corcoran/istockphoto.com (baby pandas); pg. 21 fotoVoyager/
istockphoto.com (Great Wall); pg. 21 Carmen Martínez Banús/istockphoto.
com (girl); pg. 21 Jose Luis Pelaez, Inc./Blend Images/Corbis (boy); pg. 21 Steve
Bloom Images/Alamy (panda with mother); pg. 28 Mike Harrington/Getty
Images (pick berries); pg. 28 Chris Windsor/Getty Images (eat berries); pg. 28
F. Schussler/PhotoLink/Getty Images (field); pg. 28 Nicholas Eveleigh/Getty
Images (ice cream); pg. 28 Anna Kucherova/shutterstock.com (strawberries);
pg. 28 Pixelbliss/shutterstock.com (jam); pg. 28-29 drbimages/istockphoto.
com (strawberry bkgd); pg. 29 kkgas/istockphoto.com (basket); pg. 36
imagedepotpro/istockphoto.com (twister); pg. 36-37 Galyna Andrushko/
shutterstock.com (grass bkgd); pg. 37 PLAINVIEW/istockphoto.com (water);
pg. 39 kwest/shutterstock.com (dune); pg. 39 PBorowka/shutterstock.com
(coral); pg. 39 Rich Carey/shutterstock.com (scuba); pg. 39 Ron Masessa.
istockphoto.com (turtle); pg. 39 George Clerk/istockphoto.com (dolphin);
pg. 39 cbpix/istockphoto.com (clownfish); pg. 39 Carmen Martínez Banús/
istockphoto.com (girl); pg. 39 Jose Luis Pelaez, Inc./Blend Images/Corbis
(boy); pg. 46 Norma Cornes/shutterstock.com (baby elephant); pg. 46 Gina
Smith/Shutterstock.com (elephant ball); pg. 46 Mark Massel/istockphoto.com
(elephant painting); pg. 46-47 Chris Rose/Getty Images (paint bkgd);
pg. 47 Jerry Alexander/Getty Images; pg. 54 Jason Patrick Ross/shutterstock.
com (monarch butterfly); pg. 54 Paul Tessier/istockphoto.com (butterfly
leaves); pg. 54 INTERFOTO/Alamy (butterfly tree); pg. 54-55 Darrell Gulin/
CORBIS (butterfly bkgd); pg. 55 Janis Litavnieks/istockphoto.com; pg. 57 dusko/
shutterstock.com (Himalyas); pg. 57 isoft/istockphoto.com (Everest); pg. 57
fotoVoyager/istockphoto.com (base camp); pg. 57 Danita Delimont/Alamy
(trekking); pg. 57 Carmen Martínez Banús/istockphoto.com (girl); pg. 57 Jose
Luis Pelaez, Inc./Blend Images/Corbis (boy); pg. 64-65 Eisenhut and Mayer
Wien/Getty Images (snacks); pg. 64-65 amanaimagesRF/Getty Images (fruit);
pg. 65 topseller/shutterstock.com (lemon); pg. 68 Ivonne Wierink/
shutterstock.com (potato salad); pg. 68 Kiselev Andrey Valerevich/shutterstock.
com (sushi); pg. 68 Fanfo/shutterstock.com (crepes); pg. 68 Julián Rovagnati/
shutterstock.com (ravioli); pg. 68 bonchan/shutterstock.com (stir fry); pg. 68
whitewish/istockphoto.com (kimchi); pg. 68 Lehner/istockphoto.com (tofu);
pg. 68 DNY59/istockphoto.com (taco); pg. 70 susan flashman/istockphoto.
com(kangaroo); pg. 70 Rene Bhavnani/istockphoto.com (llama); pg. 70 Anatoly
Kolodey/istockphoto.com (panda); pg. 70 Dennis Donohue/shutterstock.com
(ostrich); pg. 70 Calek/shutterstock.com (crocodile); pg. 70 Henk Bentlage/
shutterstock.com (hippo); pg. 70 juuce/istockphoto.com (koala); pg. 70 All
Canada Photos/Alamy (penguin); pg. 71 irin-k/shutterstock.com; pg. 72 Dave
Brosha Photography/Getty Images; pg. 73 Againstar/Shutterstock.com; pg. 75 akva/
shutterstock.com (river); pg. 75 Yuri Arcurs/shutterstock.com (cooking);
pg. 75 CPbackpacker/shutterstock.com (tents); pg. 75 Barbara Tripp/
shutterstock.com (rafting); pg. 75 Inge Johnsson/Alamy (GrandCanyon); pg. 75
Carmen Martínez Banús/istockphoto.com (girl); pg. 75 Jose Luis Pelaez, Inc./
Blend Images/Corbis (boy).

*Text Design:* Molly K. Scanlon

*Cover Design:* Susan Sanguily

*Cover Illustrator:* Daniel Griffo

# Table of Contents

Kate

Andy

Jenny

Scott

Let's Talk     Let's Learn     Let's Learn More

Let's Read     Let's Review

# Let's Remember

Do you want to go skateboarding?

That's too bad.

No, thanks. I can't. I have a stomachache.

What happened?

I'm not sure. My kite was under the tree. Now it's in the tree.

# Unit 1 How Much Food?

## Let's Talk

### A Listen and say. CD1 03

**Kate:** Is everything ready for the party? Are there enough pretzels?

**Jenny:** I think so. There are three bags.

**Kate:** Do we have any soda?

**Jenny:** Yes, we do.

**Kate:** How many cans of soda are there?

**Jenny:** There's only one can. We don't have enough.

**Kate:** How many cans do we need?

**Jenny:** We need twelve cans.

**Kate:** OK. See you soon!

CD1 04

> Are there enough pretzels?
>    I think so.
>    I don't think so.

# B Practice the words. Ask and answer.

1. a can of tomatoes    2. cans of beans    3. a bag of potato chips    4. bags of pretzels

  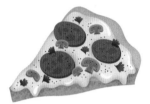 

5. a bottle of water    6. bottles of soda    7. a piece of pizza    8. pieces of watermelon

CD1 06

**How many** cans of tomatoes **are there?**
There is one can.
There are three cans.

# C Listen and sing. CD1 07

## One Piece of Pizza

Oh, there is one piece of pizza.
There are pretzels in a bag,
One piece of pizza,
Pretzels in a bag.

Oh, there are three cans of soda,
Pretzels in a bag,
Four bags of potato chips.
Oh, I love parties!

Pizza, pizza,
Is there enough pizza?
  Yes, there is.
  There's enough pizza.
There are enough pieces of pizza.
There's plenty of pizza pie. YES!

# Let's Learn

## A Learn the words. CD1 08

1. a lot of nuts

2. a few nuts

3. a lot of cupcakes

4. a few cupcakes

5. a lot of blueberries

6. a few blueberries

7. a lot of cherries

8. a few cherries

## B Make sentences. CD1 09

Jenny and Kate are getting food ready for a party. Do they have enough food?

There are a lot of nuts.
There are a few cupcakes.

How many sandwiches are there?

There are | a lot of | sandwiches.
           | a few    |

Are there a lot of cookies?
    Yes, there are.    No, there aren't.

# Let's Learn More

## A Learn the words. CD1 12

1. a lot of pudding

2. a little pudding

3. a lot of fruit

4. a little fruit

5. a lot of lemonade

6. a little lemonade

7. a lot of pie

8. a little pie

## B Ask and answer. CD1 13

Scott and Andy are at the party, too.
They are helping with the food.

How much fruit is there?
There is a lot of fruit.

How much pie is there?
There is a little pie.

# C Ask and answer. CD1 14

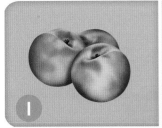 1

 2

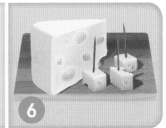 5

 4 (6)

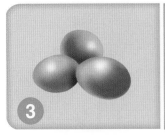 3

 4

 7

 8

How many peaches are there?

There are | a lot of / a few | peaches.

How much yogurt is there?

There is | a lot of / a little | yogurt.

# D Listen and chant. CD1 15

## Is There a Lot of Milk?

Is there a lot of milk?
   Yes, there is.
   There are bottles and bottles
   and bottles of milk.

Is there a lot of popcorn?
   There's a little popcorn.

Are there a lot of pancakes?
   No, there aren't.

Are there a lot of grapes?
   There are a few.

How many grapes?
   One or two.

# Let's Read

# DINOSAURS

Dinosaurs lived millions of years ago. There were a lot of dinosaurs then. What did they eat? Did they buy bags of dinosaur food? Did they eat pieces of bread? No!

Scientists studied dinosaur teeth. The scientists learned many things. For example, many dinosaurs ate plants. Some dinosaurs ate meat.

Apatosaurus: plant-eater

Tyrannosaurus: meat-eater

Scientists studied bones, too. Many dinosaurs had big, long bones. They were tall. They could reach the leaves on trees, but they couldn't jump. Some dinosaurs had little, short bones. They could climb trees.

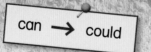
can → could

**New Words**
dinosaurs
millions of years ago
plants
meat

**B** **Choose the correct answer.** (CD1 17)

1. What did dinosaurs eat?     a. a few pieces of bread    b. a lot of plants and meat

2. Could tall dinosaurs jump?    a. No, they couldn't.    b. Yes, they could.

# C Understand the vocabulary.

> They could reach the leaves on trees.

What does reach mean?

a.

b.

c.

# D Ask your partner.

1. When did dinosaurs live?

2. What did scientists study?

3. What did scientists learn from dinosaur bones?

# E Listen and write. Do you hear mp or mb? CD1 18

1. ju_____    2. cli_____    3. la_____    4. co_____

# F Learn about words. Read and write.

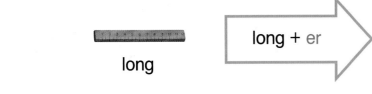

long    long + er    longer

1. short ⟶ _____    2. tall ⟶ _____

## A Listen and say. CD1 19

**Andy:** Did you know that a zebra is slower than a gazelle?

**Scott:** Really? I didn't know that.

**Andy:** Which animal is faster? A cat or a polar bear?

**Scott:** I'm not sure. I think a polar bear is probably faster.

**Andy:** No! A cat is as fast as a polar bear!

**Scott:** Wow! Are you sure? That's interesting!

**Andy:** A man is faster than a skunk.

**Scott:** Are you sure?

**Andy:** Yes, I'm sure. Look!

**Scott:** That's good! He can run away!

CD1 20

Are you sure?
Yes, I'm sure.
No, I'm not sure.

**B** **Practice the words. Ask and answer.** (CD1 21)

1. a wolf
64 kph

2. a zebra
64 kph

3. a cheetah
114 kph

4. a gazelle
80 kph

5. a rhinoceros
43 kph

6. a polar bear
43 kph

7. a squirrel
19 kph

8. a skunk
12 kph

(CD1 22)

Is a wolf as fast as a zebra?
Yes, it is.   No, it isn't. It's slower.

fast → as fast as → faster than
slow → as slow as → slower than

**C** **Listen and chant.** (CD1 23) 🎵

## A Gazelle Is as Fast as a Lion

A gazelle is as fast
as a lion.
But a lion is smarter
than a cow.

You're probably right,
but I'm not sure.
Is a lion smarter
than a cow?

A rhino is bigger than
a zebra.
But it's smaller than a
polar bear.

You're probably right,
but I'm not sure.
Is it smaller than
a polar bear?

Some skunks are as little
as squirrels.
Some skunks are as big
as cats.

You're probably right,
but I'm not sure.
Is a skunk as big as
a cat?

**Unit 2** Comparing Animals   **13**

# Let's Learn

## A  Learn the words. (CD1 24)

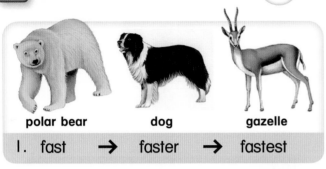

polar bear · dog · gazelle

1. fast → faster → fastest

squirrel · skunk · turtle

2. slow → slower → slowest

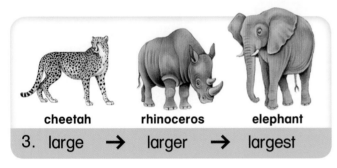

cheetah · rhinoceros · elephant

3. large → larger → largest

puppy · kitten · mouse

4. small → smaller → smallest

## B  Ask and answer. (CD1 25)

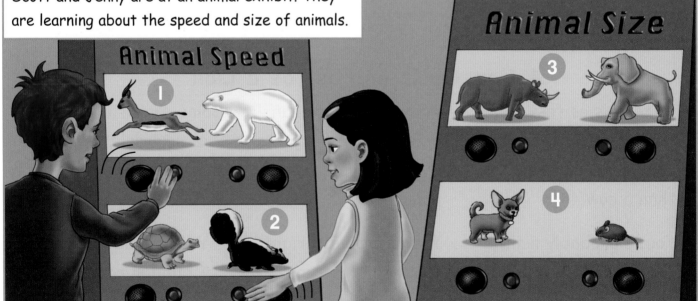

Scott and Jenny are at an animal exhibit. They are learning about the speed and size of animals.

Animal Speed

Animal Size

Which one is faster?
The gazelle is faster. The gazelle is faster than the polar bear.

## C Ask and answer.  CD1 26

| 1. fast | 2. slow | 3. large | 4. small |
|---------|---------|----------|----------|

cheetah

polar bear

zebra

cat

wolf

turtle

lion

rhinoceros

cow

mouse

skunk

squirrel

> Which one is the fastest?
> The cheetah is the fastest.

## D Listen and chant.  CD1 27

### Cheetah Chant

A greyhound is fast,
Faster than a cat,
But a cheetah is the fastest of all.

A racehorse is fast,
Faster than a fox,
But a cheetah is the fastest of all.

A rabbit is fast,
Faster than a cat,
But a cheetah is the fastest of all.

A rabbit is faster
  than a baby kangaroo,
But a cheetah is the fastest of all.

## A Learn the words. CD1 28

1. colorful     2. graceful     3. expensive     4. delicious

## B Say these. CD1 29

| The polar bear is the least colorful. | The squirrel is less colorful than the frog. | The frog is colorful. | The fish is more colorful than the frog. | The bird is the most colorful. |
|---|---|---|---|---|

## C Ask and answer. CD1 30

Kate and Jenny are in the zoo gift shop. They are comparing gifts.

Which one is more colorful?
The fish is more colorful.

Which one is less colorful?
The frog is less colorful.

Which one is the most graceful?
The gazelle is the most graceful.

Which one is the least graceful?
The elephant is the least graceful.

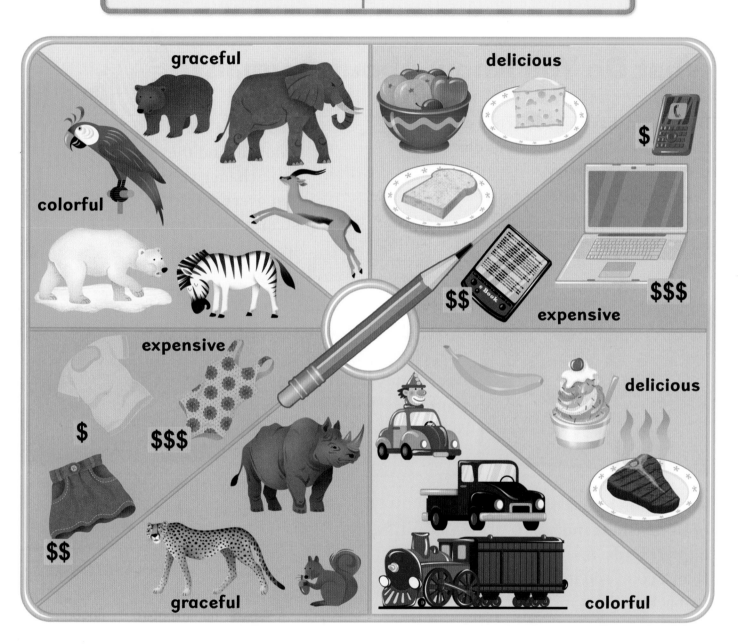

graceful

delicious

colorful

$

$$

expensive

$$$

expensive

$

$$$

$$

graceful

delicious

$$$

colorful

**E** Ask and answer. Look at the pictures in **D**. (CD1 32)

Is the skirt more expensive than the shirt?
Yes, it is.
No, it isn't.

# Let's Read

## A  Listen and read along. Then read again. (CD1 33)

# What Do You Know About Animals?

Polar bears have a good sense of smell. They can smell fish under the ice from far away. They are strong, and they can smash open ice blocks to catch the fish.

Zebras are not colorful, and they can't change color. But every zebra's stripes are different, just like fingerprints.

The mimic octopus isn't colorful. But it can change its color and shape. It can look like a jellyfish, a snake, or fifteen different animals.

A box jellyfish has 24 eyes. It is shaped like a box.

A hummingbird is one of the smallest and lightest birds. It is lighter than a coin, and it can fly backwards.

### New Words

| | |
|---|---|
| smash | change |
| hummingbird | fingerprints |
| backwards | jellyfish |
| mimic octopus | shape |

## B  Choose the correct answer. (CD1 34)

1. What animal can change color and shape?    a. a jellyfish    b. a mimic octopus

2. Is a coin heavier than a hummingbird?    a. Yes, it is.    b. No, it isn't.

## **C** Understand the vocabulary.

It can look like fifteen different animals.

What does look like mean?

a.

b.

c.

## **D** Ask your partner.

1. What bird can fly backwards?

2. Which animal is the most interesting? Why?

## **E** Listen and write. Do you hear ar or ir?  (CD1 35)

1. b_____d    2. sc_____f    3. th_____d    4. c_____d    5. sh_____k

## **F** Learn about words. Read and write.

 small    small + est    smallest

1. light ⟶ _____    2. slow ⟶ _____

3. tall ⟶ _____    4. strong ⟶ _____

# Let's Review

## A Listen and check. CD1 36

1.

A ☐　　　B ☐　　　C ☐

2.

A ☐　　　B ☐　　　C ☐

3.

A ☐　　　B ☐　　　C ☐

4.

A ☐　　　B ☐　　　C ☐

## B Listen and circle. CD1 37

1.　a. It's slower.　　b. It's faster.　　　　2.　a. It's larger.　　b. It's smaller.

## C Listen and check. CD1 38

1.

A ☐　　　B ☐　　　C ☐

2.

A ☐　　　B ☐　　　C ☐

3.

A ☐　　　B ☐　　　C ☐

4.

A ☐　　　B ☐　　　C ☐

## D Let's read about a panda kindergarten.

We're in China!

**John and Lisa's Travel Blog**

China

### Ni Hao from Panda Kindergarten, China!

*ni hao = hello*

This week, we're volunteering at a panda kindergarten. Every morning, we clean the pandas' rooms, and then we feed them. They eat a lot of bamboo every day! Pandas also like carrots and apples. We didn't know that.

Newborn pandas are very small. They are about as light as a stick of butter. But they grow quickly.

We like watching the pandas. They really like to play. Baby pandas like to tumble, climb, and chase. They are very funny.

#### What About You?

- How many pets do you have?

- Do you like to watch baby animals? What do they do? Are they funny?

**New Words**
kindergarten
bamboo
carrot
newborn
stick of butter
tumble

## E Write about a baby animal.

Comments

# Unit 3 Last Weekend

## Let's Talk

### A Listen and say. (CD1 40)

**Jenny:** How was your weekend?
**Scott:** It was great. How was yours?
**Jenny:** It was pretty good.

**Scott:** What did you do?
**Jenny:** My brother and I went for a bike ride.
**Scott:** That sounds like fun.

**Jenny:** What did you do last weekend?
**Scott:** I went shopping and bought this new bike.
**Jenny:** Wow! I like it.
**Scott:** Thanks.

(CD1 41)

How was your weekend?
It was great.
It was pretty good.

yours = your weekend

## B Practice the words. Ask and answer.

1. went for a walk

2. went for a bike ride

3. went for a swim

4. went bowling

5. went shopping

6. went skating

CD1 43

> What did he do last weekend?
> He went for a walk.

## C Listen and chant. CD1 44

### Last Summer, What Did You Do?

Last summer, what did you do?
  I went to Hawaii.
I did, too.
Did you buy anything?
  Yes, I did. I bought
  a two-dollar tie.
So did I.

Last winter, where did you go?
  I went to London.
So did Joe.
Did you buy anything?
  Yes, I did. I bought English tea.
So did he.

# Let's Learn

## A Learn the words. CD1 45

1. skateboarding

2. hiking

3. taking pictures

4. playing volleyball

5. running

6. walking the dogs

## B Ask and answer. CD1 46

It was Saturday. Jenny and Scott saw Kate and Andy at the park. What were they doing before?

What was Kate doing?
She **was** walking the dogs.

## C Ask and answer. CD1 47

| What was she doing yesterday?<br>She **was** walking the dog. | What were they doing yesterday?<br>They **were** hiking. |
| --- | --- |

## D Listen and chant. CD1 48

### Our Dogs

Last night, our dogs were having fun.
They were having a very good time.

What were they doing?
  They were skateboarding.
  They were having a very good time.

Your dogs were skateboarding?
  Yes, they were.
  They were having a very good time.

# Let's Learn More

## A Learn the words. CD1 49

1. buying sneakers

2. mailing a package

3. playing catch

4. watching DVDs

5. borrowing books

6. surfing the Internet

## B Ask and answer. CD1 50

It's Sunday. The children met in the park again this afternoon. Where were they this morning? What were they doing there?

| Where was Andy this morning? | What was he doing there? |
| He was at home. | He was watching DVDs. |

## C Play a game. Ask your partner. (CD1 51)

| What was she<br>What were they | doing this afternoon? | She was<br>They were | buying boots at the mall. |

## D What about you?

Where were you this morning? What were you doing?

I was _____ at _____.

## A Listen and read along. Then read again. (CD1 52)

### A Trip to the Strawberry Farm

Last weekend, I went to a strawberry farm with my family. We picked a lot of ripe, red strawberries.

*Strawberries are the only fruit with seeds on the outside.*

I was picking strawberries in one row. My brother and my parents were in the next row. I was watching my brother. Sometimes he was picking strawberries, but usually he was eating them.

We took them home and made strawberry jam and strawberry ice cream. It was fun!

### New Words
pick
ripe
row
only
seeds

## B Choose the correct answer. (CD1 53)

1. Where were they last weekend?    a. at a strawberry farm    b. at a fruit store

2. What was her brother doing?    a. buying strawberries    b. eating strawberries

## C Understand the vocabulary.

We picked a lot of ripe, red strawberries.

What does picked mean?

a.

b.

c.

## D Ask your partner.

1. Do you like strawberries?

2. Are there a lot of strawberries in your refrigerator right now?

3. What's your favorite fruit?

## E Listen and write. Do you hear st or str? CD1 54

1. _____awberry   2. _____ar   3. _____ipes   4. _____ore   5. _____ing

## F Learn about words. Read and write.

 strawberry    strawberry − y + ies    strawberries

1. family ⟶ _____    2. cherry ⟶ _____

**A** **Listen and say.** CD1 55

**Andy:** Are you ready?
**Kate:** Not yet. Wait a minute.
**Andy:** Why?
**Kate:** I think I forgot to do something.

**Andy:** Did you put on sunscreen?
**Kate:** Yes, I did. I put it on.
**Andy:** Did you turn off the radio?
**Kate:** Yes, I turned it off.
**Andy:** OK. You're ready.

**Kate:** Oh, no! Now I remember.
**Andy:** What?
**Kate:** I forgot to take off my watch.
**Andy:** I hope it's waterproof.

CD1 56

Are you ready?
    Not yet. Wait a minute.

## B Practice the words. Ask and answer.  CD1 57

1. put on sunscreen

2. turn on the TV

3. take off your watch

4. turn off the radio

5. turn in your
   homework

6. turn up the heat

7. clean up
   your room

8. turn down
   the music

CD1 58

**Did you** put on sunscreen?
   Yes, I put it on.
   No, I didn't put it on.

## C Listen and sing. CD1 59

♪ **Tom Came Home and Turned On the Radio**

Tom came home
   and turned on the radio,
Turned on the radio,
Turned on the radio.
Tom came home
   and turned on the radio.
Tom turned the radio on.

Paul came home
   and put on a DVD,
Put on a DVD,
Put on a DVD.
Paul came home
   and put on a DVD.
Paul put a DVD on.

# Let's Learn

## A Learn the words. (CD1 60)

1. walk quickly

2. walk slowly

3. speak loudly

4. speak quietly

5. paint beautifully

6. dance gracefully

## B Ask and answer. (CD1 61)

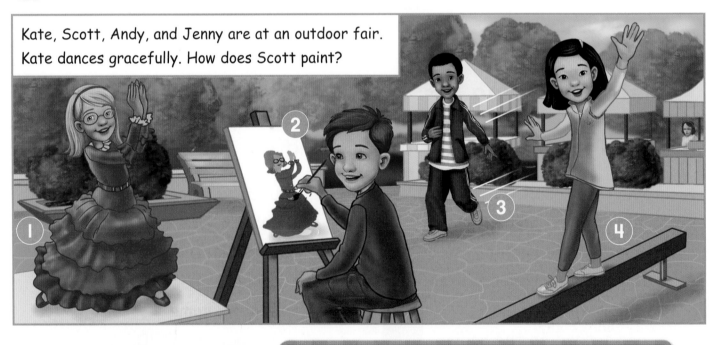

Kate, Scott, Andy, and Jenny are at an outdoor fair.
Kate dances gracefully. How does Scott paint?

How does Kate dance?
She dances gracefully.

| | | | |
|---|---|---|---|
| quick | → quickly | quiet | → quietly |
| slow | → slowly | beautiful | → beautifully |
| loud | → loudly | graceful | → gracefully |

## C Ask and answer.  CD1 62

1.

2.

3.

4.

5.

6.

**Does** she walk quickly?
   **Yes**, she **does**.
   **No**, she **doesn't**. She walks slowly.

## D Listen and chant. CD1 63

### My Friend Joe Is Very Slow

My friend Joe is very slow.
He talks slowly, very slowly.
He walks slowly, very slowly.
Hurry up, Joe, let's go!

My friend Rick is very quick.
He talks quickly, very quickly.
He walks quickly, very quickly.
Slow down, Rick. Slow down!

My friend Joe is very slow.
He eats slowly, very slowly.
He works slowly, very slowly.
He drives slowly, very slowly.
Hurry up, Joe. Let's go!

My friend Rick is very quick.
He eats quickly, very quickly.
He works quickly, very quickly.
He drives quickly, very quickly.
Slow down, Rick. Slow down!

# Let's Learn More

## A Learn the words. CD1 64

1. play the guitar

Hello!

2. speak English

3. ride a unicycle

4. bake

5. cook

6. sew

## B Ask and answer. CD1 65

Kate, Jenny, Scott, and Andy are in a show.
What do they do well?

What does Kate do well?   She sews very well.

## C Play a game. Make sentences. (CD1 66)

She speaks English **very** well.

A
talks
dances
walks
paints
plays
speaks
rides
bakes

B
quickly    slowly
quietly    loudly
gracefully
beautifully
well

Nice to meet you.

## D What about you?

Do you speak loudly or quietly?
Do you walk quickly or slowly?
What do you do well?

**A** Listen and read along. Then read again.

# A Tornado in a Bottle

A tornado is a storm. In this storm, the wind moves very quickly in a circle. Tornadoes can pick up trees, cars, and houses!

You can make a model tornado in a bottle. Here's how to do it.

1. Use two bottles. Put water in one of the bottles, Put tape on the mouth of the bottle. Make a hole.

2. Tape the necks of the bottles tightly together.

3. Turn over the bottles. Tilt the bottles and swirl the water in a circle. You are going to see a little tornado.

**New Words**

| | |
|---|---|
| tornado | hole |
| storm | tightly |
| wind | tilt |
| model | swirl |

**B** Choose the correct answer. CD1 68

1. Does a tornado move slowly?     a. Yes, it does.    b. No, it doesn't.
   It moves very slowly.    It moves quickly.

2. What can a tornado do?    a. pick up houses    b. fill bottles with water

##  C Understand the vocabulary.

> Tilt the bottles and swirl the water in a circle.

What does swirl mean?

a.     b.     c.

## D Ask your partner.

1. What is a tornado?

2. How does a tornado move?

## E Listen and write. Do you hear lt or ld? CD1 69

1. ti_____    2. co_____    3. qui_____    4. o_____    5. be_____

## F Learn about words. Read and write.

 tight     tight + ly   ⟹   tightly

1. quick ⟶ _____     2. loud ⟶ _____

3. soft ⟶ _____     4. slow ⟶ _____

# Let's Review ✓

## A Listen and number. (CD1 70)

a

b

c

d

## B Listen and check. (CD1 71)

1.

A ☐    B ☐    C ☐

2.

A ☐    B ☐    C ☐

3.

A ☐   B ☐

4.

A ☐   B ☐

We're in Australia!

## John and Lisa's Travel Blog

Great Barrier Reef, Australia

## *G'day* from the Great Barrier Reef in Australia!

Today we went scuba diving. We swam slowly around the coral and saw some clownfish. They were very colorful and friendly.

Then we saw a big sea turtle. Turtles are not graceful on land, but they are very graceful in the water.

We swam back to the boat. Dolphins swam next to us and jumped out of the water.

This is the world's largest coral reef. It's a beautiful underwater world!

*g'day = good day*

### *What About You?*

- Can you swim underwater?
- What can you see underwater?

### New Words

scuba diving
coral reef
clownfish
underwater

## **D** Write about a water activity.

Comments

**A** Listen and say. CD2 02

**Kate:** What do you think you'll be when you grow up?
**Jenny:** I think I'll be a tennis player.
**Kate:** Good idea! You play tennis very well.

**Kate:** What about me? What do you think I'll be?
**Jenny:** Hmm. Maybe you'll be an engineer.
**Kate:** Really? I don't think so. I hate math.

**Kate:** I think I'll be a designer.
**Jenny:** You're probably right. You're really good at drawing.
**Kate:** Maybe I'll make a tennis outfit for you.
**Jenny:** That'll be great! Thanks.

CD2 03

I think I'll be a tennis player.
Good idea!
You're probably right.

you will = you'll
I will = I'll
That will = That'll

## B Practice the words. CD2 04

1. a tennis
   player
2. a movie
   director
3. a designer
4. a hair
   stylist
5. a surgeon
6. a flight
   attendant

## C Ask and answer.

CD2 05

> What do you think he'll be?
> I think he'll be a hair stylist.

> he will = he'll
> she will = she'll

## D Listen and chant. CD2 06 ♪♫

### What Will Lynn Be?

Will Lynn be a lawyer?
  No, I don't think so.

Will she be a doctor?
  No, I don't think so.

She won't be a lawyer.
She won't be a doctor.

What do you think she'll be?
  I think she'll be an English teacher.

We'll see!

# Let's Learn

## A Learn the words.  CD2 07

1. do the laundry

2. set the table

3. make the bed

4. dust the furniture

5. mop the floor

6. wash the car

## B Ask and answer. CD2 08

It's Saturday. Will Jenny, Andy, Kate, and Scott do their chores?

1

2

3

4

Will Jenny mop the floor?
Yes, she will.   No, she won't.

will not = won't

## C Ask and answer.  CD2 09

1.

2.

3.

4.

5.

6.

> What will she do next?
> She'll **probably** do the laundry.

> they will = they'll
> he will = he'll
> she will = she'll

## D Listen and chant.  CD2 10 ♪♫

### Will He Hit a Home Run?

Will he hit a home run?
  He probably won't.

Do the Reds play well?
  No, they don't.

Who will score a run?
  Maybe Bill.

Will the Blue Boys win?
  They probably will.

# Let's Learn More

## A Learn the words. CD2 11

1. do homework

2. wash the dishes

3. clean my desk

4. set the alarm

5. go fishing

6. go swimming

7. go bowling

8. go to sleep

## B Ask and answer. CD2 12

Kate, Jenny, Andy, and Scott are talking about what they will do after class.

What will you do after class?
I think I'll go to sleep after class.

He **probably won't** do homework.
They'll **probably** go fishing.

**D** **What about you?**

What will you do after class?

I'll probably _____. I probably won't _____.

## A Listen and read along. Then read again. CD2 14

# ELEPHANT CAMP

Today I went to an elephant camp in Thailand. The elephants and their trainers were playing soccer! They were very good. The elephants can play soccer better than I can!

Another elephant was painting a picture. Her name was Sai. She wrapped her trunk around the paintbrush. She painted a picture of a flower. Sai can paint better than I can!

I visited the elephant nursery, too. The baby elephants were very cute. They played all day. Maybe they'll be soccer players or painters someday!

**New Words**

another
wrapped
nursery
cute
painters

## B Choose the correct answer. CD2 15

1. Where did he go?              a. to a zoo       b. to a camp

2. What did the baby elephants do all day?    a. They painted.   b. They played.

## C Understand the vocabulary.

> She wrapped her trunk around the paintbrush.

What does wrapped her trunk around mean?

a.

b.

c.

## D Ask your partner.

1. Can elephants paint pictures?

2. Where were the baby elephants?

## E Listen and write. Do you hear wr or wh? CD2 16

1. _____ite

2. _____ap

3. _____ite

4. _____ale

## F Learn about words. Read and write.

 paint

 brush

paint + brush ➔ paintbrush

1. homework = _____ + _____

2. sunglasses = _____ + _____

3. snowboard = _____ + _____

4. jellyfish = _____ + _____

**A** **Listen and say.** CD2 17

**Scott:** Summer is my favorite season.
**Andy:** Why?
**Scott:** Because it's hot and there's no school.

**Scott:** What's your favorite season?
**Andy:** Winter.
**Scott:** Why?
**Andy:** Because I like skiing.

**Scott:** I like skiing, too ... waterskiing!
**Andy:** That sounds like fun. Let's go waterskiing this summer!

CD2 18

I like waterskiing.
That sounds like fun.

### Did You Know?

Summer in the Northern Hemisphere is usually June, July, and August. Summer in the Southern Hemisphere is usually December, January, and February.

## B Practice the words. Ask and answer.

1. ice skating    2. skiing

3. planting flowers    4. flying kites

5. going to the beach    6. waterskiing

7. camping    8. picking apples

Why do you like winter?
I like winter because I like ice skating.

## C Listen and chant. CD2 21

### What's Your Favorite Season?

What's your favorite season?
  I love winter.
I don't like winter at all.
  Why do you hate winter?
Because I hate the cold.
I like spring or fall.

What's your favorite season?
  I love summer.
I don't like summer at all.
  Why do you hate summer?
Because I hate the heat.
I don't like summer at all.

# Let's Learn

## A Learn the words. CD2 22

1. went backpacking

2. raked leaves

3. went sledding

4. had a snowball fight

5. had a picnic

6. picked flowers

7. went swimming

8. built a sandcastle

## B Ask and answer. CD2 23

Andy, Kate, Scott, and Jenny are showing photos of what they did last weekend.

What did you do last weekend?
I built a sandcastle.

## C Ask and answer.  CD2 24

**Weekend Activities**

What did he do last weekend?
He went backpacking.

## D Listen and sing. CD2 25

### What Did You Do?

What did you do?
Where did you go?
Who did you see last night?
Please tell me.
What did you do?
Where did you go?
  I had fun last night.
Oh, what did you do?
Where did you go?

I had a wonderful time.
I stayed home and did my homework.
I had a wonderful time.

# Let's Learn More

## A Learn the words. (CD2 26)

1. go trekking

2. go to a water park

3. go rafting

4. go to a baseball game

5. go scuba diving

6. go surfing

7. go snowboarding

8. go horseback riding

## B Make sentences. (CD2 27)

Andy, Scott, Jenny, and Kate are planning their next vacations. What will they do?

Andy **will probably** go surfing.

## C Ask and answer. (CD2 28)

1.

last summer

next summer

2.

last winter

next winter

3.

last spring

next spring

4.

last fall

next fall

| What did he do last summer? | What will he do next summer? |
| He went to a water park. | He'll probably go scuba diving. |

## D What about you?

What did you do last summer?

What did you do last month?

What will you do next summer?

What will you do tomorrow?

# Let's Read

**A** **Listen and read along. Then read again.** (CD2 29)

# Butterflies

The monarch butterflies are here in California! They usually live in the north in the summer. Every winter, they spread their wings and fly south to Mexico because they don't like the cold.

In the winter, the butterflies stop in California to rest. They are in all the trees. Winter is my favorite season because the butterflies are here. They are graceful, colorful, and wonderful.

Monarch butterflies are beautiful. They fill the sky with orange and black spots when they fly.

In the spring, they will fly north again to Canada.

**New Words**

monarch butterfly
north
spread
wings
south
wonderful

**B** **Choose the correct answer** (CD2 30)

1. Where do monarch butterflies usually live?  a. in the north   b. in the south
2. Where will the butterflies go in the spring?  a. north   b. south

## C Understand the vocabulary.

They spread their wings and fly.

What does spread mean?

a.

b.

c.

## D Ask your partner.

1. Why do the butterflies fly south in the winter?

2. What's your favorite season? Why?

## E Listen and write. Do you hear spr or sp? CD2 31

Hello.

1. _____ot    2. _____ing    3. _____aghetti    4. _____ead    5. _____eak

## F Learn about words. Read and write.

 color    color + ful    colorful

1. grace  _____    2. wonder  _____

# Let's Review ✓

1.

A ☐   B ☐   C ☐

2.

A ☐   B ☐   C ☐

3.

A ☐   B ☐   C ☐

4.

A ☐   B ☐   C ☐

5.

A ☐   B ☐   C ☐

6.

A ☐   B ☐   C ☐

7.

A ☐   B ☐   C ☐

8.

A ☐   B ☐   C ☐

## B Let's read about Mt. Everest. (CD2 33)

We're in Nepal!

**John and Lisa's Travel Blog**

Mt. Everest, Nepal

# *Namaste* from Mt. Everest, Nepal!

namaste = hello

We're not at the top of Mt. Everest because only mountain climbers can go there. But we can see the top!

We stayed with a host family in a small village last night. Everyone was very friendly. We ate curry and bread for dinner. It was delicious.

Summer is trekking season. It's too cold in the winter. Tomorrow, our guides will take us to the Everest Base Camp. We'll be at the top of the world!

### *What About You?*

- What did you do last weekend? Did you go trekking in the mountains?

- Do you think you'll eat curry for dinner? What will you probably eat for dinner?

### New Words
Mt. Everest
host family
village
curry

## C Write about your visit to a new place.

Comments

**A** Listen and say. CD2 34

| | |
|---|---|
| **Scott:** | Something smells good. What are you doing? |
| **Kate:** | I'm baking cookies. |
| **Scott:** | Are they done? |
| **Kate:** | Almost. |

| | |
|---|---|
| **Kate:** | Oh, no. |
| **Scott:** | What happened? |
| **Kate:** | I don't know. They don't look good. |
| **Scott:** | They smell good. I'll try one. |

| | |
|---|---|
| **Kate:** | How is it? |
| **Scott:** | It tastes great! |

CD2 35

What happened?
I don't know.

## B Say these. (CD2 36)

1.  Look at the butterfly.
It looks beautiful.

2.  Listen to the music.
It sounds wonderful.

3.  Smell the flower.
It smells good.

4.  Touch the rabbit.
It feels soft.

5.  Taste the candy.
It tastes sweet.

## C Practice the words. Make sentences. (CD2 37)

1. sunset

2. bird

3. rose

4. pillow

5. strawberry

(CD2 38)

Look at **the** sunset.
It looks beautiful.

## D Listen and chant. (CD2 39)

### Listen! Do You Hear That Music?

Listen! Do you hear that music?
Yes, I do. It sounds beautiful!

Look! Do you see that rainbow?
Yes, I do. It looks amazing!

Taste these cookies. They taste good.
Mmmmm. They're delicious!

Smell the roses. They smell sweet.
Mmmmm. They smell wonderful!

Touch this pillow. It feels soft.
Mmmmm. It feels nice!

# Let's Learn

## A Learn the words. (CD2 40)

1. rainbow / beautiful

2. mask / ugly

3. music / wonderful

4. noise / awful

5. garbage / bad

6. soap / good

## B Make sentences. (CD2 41)

Kate, Jenny, Scott, and Andy are using their senses.
How do the things around them look, sound, and smell?

The rainbow looks beautiful.

| look | → | looks |
| sound | → | sounds |
| smell | → | smells |

## C Ask and answer. CD2 42

1. butterfly / beautiful

2. garbage / bad

3. noise / awful

4. mask / ugly

5. music / wonderful

6. rose / good

How does the butterfly look?
It looks beautiful.

## D Listen and chant. CD2 43

### I Smell Smoke

I smell smoke.
Something's burning.
It smells terrible.
It smells awful.

I see a horse.
Somebody's riding.
It looks wonderful.
It looks beautiful.

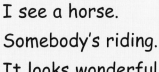
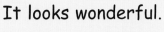

I hear music.
Somebody's singing.
It sounds wonderful.
It sounds beautiful.

I hear English.
Somebody's speaking.
It sounds interesting.
It sounds beautiful.

# Let's Learn More

## A Learn the words. (CD2 44)

|  1. pillow / soft |  2. rock / hard |  3. mirror / smooth |  4. tree / rough |

|  5. honey / sweet |  6. lemon / sour |  7. potato chip / salty |  8. dark chocolate / bitter |

## B Ask and answer. (CD2 45)

Jenny and Andy went to a day care center. They talked with the children about the senses.

How does the mirror feel?
The mirror feels smooth.

| feel | → | feels |
| taste | → | tastes |

## C Play a game. Ask and answer. (CD2 46)

> Does it feel rough or smooth?
> It feels rough.

## D Ask your partner. (CD2 47)

> Which do you like better, salty food or sweet food?
> I like salty food better.

1. salty food or sweet food?

2. loud music or quiet music?

3. sweet chocolate or bitter chocolate?

4. a soft pillow or a hard pillow?

## A Listen and read along. Then read again. CD2 48

### Why Do Foods Taste Different?

You need two things to taste food: taste buds and a sense of smell.

Taste buds are on your tongue. They help you taste each kind of flavor. Taste buds tell you that ice cream is sweet, potato chips are salty, lemons are sour, and some dark chocolate is bitter.

Your sense of smell is important, too. It helps you taste.

Try this. Drink a glass of apple juice. It will taste sweet. Then pinch your nose closed. Drink some more juice. Now you can't taste it because you can't smell it.

Sweet

Sour

Bitter

Salty

**New Words**

| | |
|---|---|
| taste buds | flavor |
| sense | pinch |
| tongue | |

## B Choose the correct answer. CD2 49

1. Where are your taste buds?　　　　a. on your nose　　b. on your tongue

2. Can you taste food when you pinch your nose?　　　　a. Yes, you can.　　b. No, you can't.

## C Understand the vocabulary.

> Pinch your nose closed.

What does pinch mean?

a.

b.

c.

## D Ask your partner.

1. Why do foods taste different?

2. What's your favorite flavor? Why?

## E Listen and write. Do you hear nch or ch? (CD2 50)

1. pi_____    2. rea_____    3. lu_____    4. pea_____

## F Learn about words. Read and write.

 salt ⟹ salt + y ⟹ salty

1. rain ⟶ _____    2. snow ⟶ _____
3. cloud ⟶ _____    4. wind ⟶ _____

## Let's Talk

### A Listen and say. (CD2 51)

**Jenny:** Guess what!
**Scott:** What?
**Jenny:** I'm going to go to France this summer.
**Scott:** That's exciting!

**Scott:** Have you been there before?
**Jenny:** No. It's my first time.
**Scott:** I've been there twice. My uncle lives there. I visited him last summer.

**Jenny:** Wow! You're lucky! I don't know anyone there.
**Scott:** You'll love France!
**Jenny:** There's only one problem. I don't speak French!

(CD2 52)

Have you been there before?
No. It's my first time.
Yes. I've been there twice.

be ⟶ been

## B Practice the words. Ask and answer. CD2 53

1. Egypt

2. China

3. Hawaii

4. Nepal

5. the Grand Canyon

6. Mt. Everest

7. France

8. the Great Barrier Reef

CD2 54
> Have you ever been to Egypt?
> Yes, I have.   No, I haven't.

## C Listen and chant. CD2 55

### Have You Ever?

Have you ever climbed
Mt. Everest?
　Yes, I have.
　I loved it.
　You will, too.

Have you ever been
to China?
　Yes, I have.
　I loved it.
　You will, too.

Have you ever been to Egypt?
　No, I haven't.

Have you ever been to Hawaii?
　No, I haven't.

I've been there and everywhere.
I loved it.
You will, too.

# Let's Learn

## A Learn the words. CD2 56

1. fried noodles

2. potato salad

3. sushi

4. ravioli

5. crepes

6. kimchi

7. tofu

8. tacos

## B Ask and answer. CD2 57

Kate and Andy are talking about foods they have eaten. They want to taste new foods.

Have you ever eaten sushi?
Yes, I have.    No, I haven't.

eat → eaten

## C Make sentences. (CD2 58)

I've eaten crepes.
I've never eaten kimchi.

I have → I've

## D Listen, point, and chant. (CD2 59) ♪♫

### Have You Ever Eaten Sushi?

Have you ever eaten sushi?
  No, I haven't, but I'll try it tonight.
All right.

Have you ever eaten tacos?
  No, I haven't, but I'll try them
  tonight.
All right.

Have you ever eaten tofu?
  Yes, I have.

Have you ever eaten crepes?
    Yes, I have.
    But I've never eaten sushi.
    And I've never eaten tacos.
    I'll try them tonight.
All right.

# Let's Learn More

## A Learn the words. CD2 60

1. a crocodile

2. an ostrich

3. a panda

4. a penguin

5. a llama

6. a kangaroo

7. a koala

8. a hippopotamus

## B Ask and answer. CD2 61

Scott and Jenny are talking about animals they have seen. Scott has seen a crocodile and a penguin. Jenny has seen a panda, an ostrich, and a kangaroo.

Have you ever seen a crocodile?
Yes, I have.
No, I haven't.

see → seen

## C Play a game. Ask and answer. (CD2 62)

Has she ever seen a crocodile?
Yes, she has.   No, she hasn't.

seen
been
eaten

START

EGYPT

✓

✓

✓

✓

X

?

X

PARIS

END

X

## D What about you? (CD2 63)

1.

2.

3.

4.

I've been to Hawaii.
I've never been to Hawaii.

## A Listen and read along. Then read again. (CD2 64)

# The Dream Catcher

Do you ever have bad dreams at night? Native Americans believe that a dream catcher can catch your unhappy dreams. Then you will only have happy dreams. Have you ever seen a dream catcher? It looks like a spider's web.

You can make a dream catcher. Here is how to do it.

**New Words**

dream
Native Americans
spider's web
weave
hang down
tie
feather

feathers

beads

a paper plate

yarn

1.  Cut out the center of a paper plate. Around the plate, make holes about 1 cm apart.

3.  Now weave across the plate. A few pieces of yarn can hang down. Put beads on the yarn.

2.  Put yarn into one hole. Then weave the yarn from hole to hole, up and over, around the plate.

4.  Finally, tie feathers to the yarn. Hang your dream catcher on the wall. Sweet dreams!

## B Choose the correct answer. (CD2 65)

1. What does a dream catcher look like?    a. a paper plate    b. a spider's web

2. What does a dream catcher do?    a. It catches happy dreams.    b. It catches unhappy dreams.

## C Understand the vocabulary.

Cut out the center of a paper plate.

What does cut out the center mean?

a.

b.

c.

## D Ask your partner.

1. Have you ever seen a dream catcher?

2. Do you remember your dreams?

## E Listen and write. Do you hear tch or t? CD2 66

1. pu_____    2. ca_____    3. ca_____    4. hopsco_____

## F Learn about words. Read and write.

    happy    un + happy    unhappy

1. friendly ⟶ _____    2. do ⟶ _____

3. wrap ⟶ _____    4. sure ⟶ _____

# Let's Review ✓

## A Listen and number. (CD2 67)

a

b

c

d

e

f

g

h

## B Listen and check. (CD2 68)

| | Jenny | | Andy | |
|---|---|---|---|---|
| | Yes | No | Yes | No |
| 1. eaten tacos | | | | |
| 2. been to Hawaii | | | | |
| 3. seen a crocodile | | | | |

## C Let's read about the Grand Canyon.

We're in the U.S.A.!

**John and Lisa's Travel Blog**

Grand Canyon, U.S.A.

## *Hello* from the Grand Canyon, U.S.A.!

This morning, we went rafting on the Colorado River. The river goes through the Grand Canyon. We went through a lot of rapids. They were very rough. We've never gone rafting before. It was exciting.

In the afternoon, we camped near the river. For dinner, the guides cooked steaks over a campfire. The steaks smelled and tasted delicious!

Tonight we're going to sleep outside. We can hear the river. It sounds wonderful. We can also see a lot of stars. We've never seen so many stars!

### *What About You?*

- Have you ever gone rafting?
- Have you ever cooked over a campfire?

**New Words**

Colorado River
rapids
campfire

## D Write about a new experience.

Comments

# Let's Go 5 Syllabus

## Unit 1  How Much Food?

| Let's Talk | Let's Learn | Let's Learn More | Let's Read |
|---|---|---|---|
| **Conversation:** Is everything ready for the party? Are there enough pretzels? I think so. How many cans of soda are there? There is only one can. How many cans do we need? We need twelve cans.<br><br>**Food:** a can of tomatoes, cans of beans, a bag of potato chips, bags of pretzels, a bottle of water, bottles of soda, a piece of pizza, pieces of watermelon<br><br>**Song:** One Piece of Pizza | **Quantities of Food:** a lot of/a few nuts, a lot of/a few cupcakes, a lot of/a few blueberries, a lot of/a few cherries<br><br>**Language:** There are a lot of nuts. There are a few cupcakes. How many sandwiches are there? There are a lot of/a few sandwiches. | **Quantities of Food:** a lot of/a little pudding, a lot of/a little fruit, a lot of/a little lemonade, a lot of/a little pie<br><br>**Language:** How much fruit is there? There is a lot of fruit. There is a little pie. How many peaches are there?<br><br>**Chant:** Is There a Lot of Milk? | **Descriptive Article:** Dinosaurs<br><br>**Questions**<br><br>**Vocabulary:** reach<br><br>**Phonics: mp** jump<br>　　　**mb** climb<br><br>**Word Study:**<br>long + er = longer |

## Unit 2  Comparing Animals

| Let's Talk | Let's Learn | Let's Learn More | Let's Read |
|---|---|---|---|
| **Conversation:** Did you know that a zebra is slower than a gazelle? Which animal is faster? A cat or a polar bear? I'm not sure. A cat is as fast as a polar bear! Are you sure? Yes, I'm sure.<br><br>**Animals:** a wolf, a zebra, a cheetah, a gazelle, a rhinoceros, a polar bear, a squirrel, a skunk<br><br>**Chant:** A Gazelle is as Fast as a Lion | **Comparatives:** fast, faster, fastest; slow, slower, slowest; large, larger, largest; small, smaller, smallest<br><br>**Language:** Which one is faster? The gazelle is faster. Which one is the fastest? The cheetah is the fastest.<br><br>**Chant:** Cheetah Chant | **Descriptions:** colorful, graceful, expensive, delicious<br><br>**Language:** Which one is more/less colorful? The fish is more colorful. The frog is less colorful. Which one is the most/the least graceful? The gazelle is the most graceful. The elephant is the least graceful. | **Article:** What Do You Know About Animals?<br><br>**Questions**<br><br>**Vocabulary:** look like<br><br>**Phonics: ir** bird<br>　　　**ar** scarf<br><br>**Word Study:**<br>small + est = smallest |

**Let's Review Units 1 and 2**　　　**Reading: John and Lisa's Travel Blog—Panda Kindergarten, China**

## Unit 3  Last Weekend

| Let's Talk | Let's Learn | Let's Learn More | Let's Read |
|---|---|---|---|
| **Conversation:** How was your weekend? It was great. How was yours? It was pretty good. What did you do? My brother and I went for a bike ride. That sounds like fun. What did you do last weekend? I went shopping and bought this new bike.<br><br>**Weekend Activities:** went for a walk/a bike ride/a swim; went bowling/shopping/skating<br><br>**Chant:** Last Summer, What Did You Do? | **Weekend Activities:** skateboarding, hiking, taking pictures, playing volleyball, running, walking the dogs<br><br>**Language:** What was Kate doing? She was walking the dogs. What was she doing yesterday? What were they doing yesterday?<br><br>**Chant:** Our Dogs | **Weekend Activities:** buying sneakers, mailing a package, playing catch, watching DVDs, borrowing books, surfing the Internet<br><br>**Language:** Where was Andy this morning? He was at home. What was he doing there? He was watching DVDs. What were they doing this afternoon? | **Informational Story:** A Trip to the Strawberry Farm<br><br>**Questions**<br><br>**Vocabulary:** picked<br><br>**Phonics: str** strawberry<br>　　　**st** star<br><br>**Word Study:** strawberry - y + ies = strawberries |

## Unit 4  Activities

| Let's Talk | Let's Learn | Let's Learn More | Let's Read |
|---|---|---|---|
| **Conversation:** Are you ready? Not yet. Wait a minute. I think I forgot to do something. Did you put on sunscreen? Yes, I put it on. Did you turn off the radio? Yes, I turned it off. Oh, no! I forgot to take off my watch.<br><br>**Routines:** put on sunscreen, turn on the TV, take off your watch, turn off the radio, turn in your homework, turn up the heat, clean up your room, turn down the music<br><br>**Song:** Tom Came Home and Turned On the Radio | **Adverbs:** walk quickly, walk slowly, speak loudly, speak quietly, paint beautifully, dance gracefully<br><br>**Language:** How does Kate dance? She dances gracefully. Does she walk quickly? Yes, she does. No, she doesn't. She walks slowly.<br><br>**Chant:** My Friend Joe Is Very Slow | **Activities:** play the guitar, speak English, ride a unicycle, bake, cook, sew<br><br>**Language:** What does Kate do well? She sews very well. She speaks English very well. | **How-To Article:** A Tornado in a Bottle<br><br>**Questions**<br><br>**Vocabulary:** swirl<br><br>**Phonics: lt** tilt<br>　　　**ld** cold<br><br>**Word Study:**<br>tight + ly = tightly |

**Let's Review Units 3 and 4**　　　**Reading: John and Lisa's Travel Blog—Great Barrier Reef, Australia**

# Unit 5  The Future

| Let's Talk | Let's Learn | Let's Learn More | Let's Read |
|---|---|---|---|
| **Conversation:** What do you think you'll be when you grow up? I think I'll be a tennis player. You play tennis very well. What do you think I'll be? Maybe you'll be an engineer. I don't think so. I think I'll be a designer. You're probably right. You're really good at drawing.<br><br>**Occupations:** a tennis player, a movie director, a designer, a hair stylist, a surgeon, a flight attendant<br><br>**Chant:** What Will Lynn Be? | **Chores:** do the laundry, set the table, make the bed, dust the furniture, mop the floor, wash the car<br><br>**Language:** Will Jenny mop the floor? Yes, she will. No, she won't. What will she do next? She'll probably do the laundry.<br><br>**Chant:** Will He Hit a Home Run? | **After School:** do homework, wash the dishes, clean my desk, set the alarm, go fishing/swimming/bowling, go to sleep<br><br>**Language:** What will you do after class? I think I'll go to sleep after class. He probably won't do homework. They'll probably go fishing. | **Photo Essay:** Elephant Camp<br><br>**Questions**<br><br>**Vocabulary:** wrapped<br>**Phonics: wr**  write<br><br>　　　　**wh**  white<br><br>**Word Study:**<br>paint + brush = paintbrush |

# Unit 6  Fun in the Seasons

| Let's Talk | Let's Learn | Let's Learn More | Let's Read |
|---|---|---|---|
| **Conversation:** Summer is my favorite season. What's your favorite season? Winter. Why? Because I like skiing. I like skiing too . . . waterskiing! That sounds like fun.<br><br>**Seasonal Activities:** winter, spring, summer, fall, ice skating, skiing, planting flowers, flying kites, going to the beach, waterskiing, camping, picking apples<br><br>**Chant:** What's Your Favorite Season? | **Seasonal Events:** went backpacking/sledding/swimming, raked leaves, had a snowball fight/picnic, picked flowers, built a sandcastle<br><br>**Language:** What did you do last weekend? I built a sandcastle. What did he do last weekend?<br><br>**Song:** What Did You Do? | **Vacation Ideas:** go trekking/rafting/scuba diving/surfing/snowboarding/horseback riding; got to a water park/baseball game<br><br>**Language:** Andy will probably go surfing. What did he do last summer? He went to a water park. What will he do next summer? | **Photo Essay:** Butterflies<br><br>**Questions**<br><br>**Vocabulary:** spread<br><br>**Phonics: sp**  spot<br>　　　　**spr**  spring<br><br>**Word Study:**<br>color + ful  = colorful |

| Let's Review Units 5 and 6 | Reading: John and Lisa's Travel Blog —Mt. Everest, Nepal |
|---|---|

# Unit 7  The Senses

| Let's Talk | Let's Learn | Let's Learn More | Let's Read |
|---|---|---|---|
| **Conversation:** Something smells good. What are you doing? I'm baking cookies. Are they done? Almost. What happened? I don't know. They don't look good. They smell good. I'll try one. How is it? It tastes great!<br><br>**Using the Senses:** look, listen, smell, touch, taste, sunset, bird, rose, pillow, strawberry<br><br>**Chant:** Listen! Do You Hear That Music? | **Senses:** rainbow/beautiful, mask/ugly, music/wonderful, noise/awful, garbage/bad, soap/good<br><br>**Language:** The rainbow looks beautiful. How does the butterfly look? It looks beautiful.<br><br>**Chant:** I Smell Smoke | **Senses:** pillow/soft, rock/hard, mirror/smooth, tree/rough, honey/sweet, lemon/sour, potato chip/salty, dark chocolate/bitter<br><br>**Language:** How does the mirror feel? The mirror feels smooth. Does it feel smooth or rough? It feels rough. | **Descriptive Article:** Why Do Foods Taste Different?<br><br>**Questions**<br><br>**Vocabulary:** pinch<br><br>**Phonics: nch** pinch<br>　　　　**ch**  reach<br><br>**Word Study:**<br>salt + y = salty |

# Unit 8  New Experiences

| Let's Talk | Let's Learn | Let's Learn More | Let's Read |
|---|---|---|---|
| **Conversation:** Guess what? I'm going to go to France this summer. Have you been there before? No. It's my first time. I've been there twice. You'll love France. There's only one problem. I don't speak French!<br><br>**Places:** Egypt, China, Hawaii, Nepal, the Grand Canyon, Mt. Everest, France, the Great Barrier Reef<br><br>**Chant:** Have You Ever? | **International Foods:** fried noodles, potato salad, sushi, ravioli, crepes, kimchi, tofu, tacos<br><br>**Language:** Have you ever eaten sushi? Yes, I have. No, I haven't. I've eaten crepes. I've never eaten kimchi.<br><br>**Chant:** Have You Ever Eaten Sushi? | **Animals from Many Places:** a crocodile, an ostrich, a panda, a penguin, a llama, a kangaroo, a koala, a hippopotamus<br><br>**Language:** Have you ever seen a crocodile? Yes, I have. No, I haven't. Has he ever seen a crocodile? Yes, she has. No, she hasn't. | **How-to Article:**<br>The Dream Catcher<br><br>**Questions**<br><br>**Vocabulary:** cut out<br><br>**Phonics: t**  put<br>　　　　**tch**  catch<br><br>**Word Study:**<br>un + happy = unhappy |

| Let's Review Units 7 and 8 | Reading: John and Lisa's Travel Blog—Grand Canyon, U.S.A. |
|---|---|

# Word List